MW00325398

www.finishinglinepress.com

Twenty-one

poems by

Katherine Barrett Swett

Finishing Line Press
Georgetown, Kentucky

Twenty-one

ACKNOWLEDGMENTS

"Label" was published in *The Mom Egg 11*

Publisher: Leah Maines

Editor: Christen Kincaid

Cover Art: Rachel Barrett Swett, 2010, www.benjaminswett.com

Author Photo: *Rachel & Katherine Swett, Fifth Station Mt. Fuji.* Photographer
    unknown.
Cover Design: Elizabeth Maines

Printed in the USA on acid-free paper.
Order online: www.finishinglinepress.com
    also available on amazon.com

Author inquiries and mail orders:
Finishing Line Press
P. O. Box 1626
Georgetown, Kentucky 40324
U. S. A.

Table of Contents

For Rachel beautiful and well favored

What we imagine

> When you were born
> I vowed
> "Till death do us part."
> My death—

Western sky

How many sundowns
will force my eyelids apart
and empty me into night?

Red eye

Jet-lagged, bag-laden, irritated, you
were meant to get off
at dawn. We are still there.

Label

I discovered on the internet fierce debate
about whether there should be a word,
like orphan, widow, for parents like us.

Routine

What dawn scatters evening brings home
to the distracted mother, but now you
are never far from my waiting mind.

Freedom

We were never to know you left
the helmet off, unveiled to the wind,
as Vermeer's maids slyly unlatch their windows.

Daisy

Before you left, I read you James's
warning to girls abroad. You leaned into
the comforting rhythm of my voice.

How it should have been that day

You finished, as planned, the final run,
catching the last patch of winter sun,
laughing, "It's ninety-five back home; it's June."

Twenty-one

This awful strength of mine keeps me—
on a too long road to you—
where another day takes me farther away.

Day job

The robin does not always sing—
with a worm dangling from her beak,
she aims to feed her young.

Morning life

I go to sleep with shades open
and sleep through dawn
into the hot midsummer light.

Source

These borrowed words would never have been
if you still were. I rarely sang—
I cannot sing—you alive.

I tell other parents

I know you imagine
your child ripped from you;
you cannot imagine not bleeding to death.

Remains

What should I do
with your soft shirts?
This is summer:
bright colors grabbed
from a dark drawer.

Visitors

Your friends are not afraid.
They enter the house unembarrassed
and take us into the emptied future.

What you wore

On the shelf black ski goggles reflect
masks of red cat, ashen Pierrette,
your face, hidden ice.

Chain

Closing the cold clasp, I cannot imagine
evenings before your arms
circled my neck, your hair shocked me.

Clasp

Is comfort grasped from gold chains
I wore years ago and gave you?
From a strand of dark hair? Whose?

On the trail

One helmetless acorn
tight in my hand, I watch summer's last
dragonfly shiver by.

Tree planting

A slender tree bending in the wind
is not a daughter bending her head,
biting her pen, writing.

Christmas dress

You sprawled in your red smocked dress
on the green chair, your electrified hair
floating like bees in the tall grass.

Gargoyle

Wild weather has eroded
the stone cherub's flower mouth
to the lipless grimace of an old man.

Twenty-one

Again and again I try to grasp—
I cannot grasp you
will never reach fifty or twenty-two.

Burial rites

Sometimes I wish we burned you
and your urn sat on the mantel
next to the forced narcissus.

Curtain calls

The dead bow from marginalia
from postcards tucked in books,
ticket stubs in linty pockets.

Alcestis

Somehow she knew it would be easier
dying for him than sorting through
all he would leave behind.

No breath at all?

Who finds consolation in outrage
at the worthless living on and on,
at the maddening perfection of butterflies?

Adaptation

Most of the world carries on.
Sparrows sing beside soggy sneakers
swinging from silver lampposts.

Bear

The cub loped across the road.
I did not see the mother—
she must be there hidden by trees.

Streams

The great heron is not blue.
She blends with rocks, trees, water
until her wings shudder, releasing the sky.

Twenty-one

You might have died an old oak,
great branches weighted down by snow,
a blast of wind.

That strain again

Had I fallen—
then there could have been requiems.
For you: no cadence.

Passing tree

How can there be a single tree
without leaves? All around it stand others
golden, green, red, brown, not bare.

Out of tune

Something catches the lutenist's eyes
as she turns the pegs; she hears the straining pitch
and a cat stretching in the sun.

Spring and fall

I have to laugh as looking back
I see what I once thought gone,
what I thought time and loneliness were.

No fall

You cannot change with the trees:
your face flowers
continuously as I walk.

Paper, scissors, rock

The grass understands the rain, and rivers
the wind, and branches the frail weight
of calling birds, and shadows all things.

No cause

Blame me.
Do not say it was
as random as trees
falling in the storm.

White lips

I cannot even howl at God
that there's no laughter
without my daughter's red mouth.

Balance sheet

Would thinking you were leant and due
back to some all-knowing debt collector
lessen grief?

Disruption

Must I remember
swollen eyes, tubes, cold skin? I cannot
remember the sound of your voice.

What I would settle for

At the very least
to hold your hand
in memory

Preliminary Theology

Your brother asks, "Did God take her?
Because if he did,
I cannot believe him."

Grammar

God is a linking verb
that takes
no objects.

Away

Some mornings for a flash I believe
you might be somewhere
about to return.

Disguise

I could wear a hat for Halloween,
become a sorceress, surpassing all those
unable to put you together again.

Twenty-one

What are the odds that someone
on this plane lost
her black-haired daughter too?

Superstition about the graveyard

Driving by, you used to hold your breath
until the white house appeared
round the curve to save you.

What happens when you look away

A quivering face peers
from the green grass by the highway.
I keep driving.

Ornery

I hope that some god can forgive all
us parents who will never forgive ourselves
every meanness in a short life.

Why don't you haunt me?

Appear in the mirror beside me brushing
your teeth, slam the door, home late,
drunk, curse my prying.

A brother's birthday

Tonight I wanted to think about you
not about your not being here tonight,
but you shaking the shadow of candles.

Four against five

In a polyrhythm, one hand
hears what the other hand is missing,
but does not follow.

Hospital bed

You lay like Saint Sebastian pierced
by tubes, eyes unseeing.
What ecstasy had you sought on that slope?

Travelers

Back home snow covers your grave
as we wander through medieval streets ignorant
of their tragedies, filling them with ours.

Girl with water pitcher

Vermeer's woman is still about to pour.
All things end, but someone goes on,
opens the window again, refills the pitcher.

Lost languages

Who would have thought my Italian
could stumble back? I make myself understood,
but cannot explain why I am still here.

Condensation

My breath ghosts as I walk
to work with you
in every step.

Lost glove

Some kind stranger stretched on the spikes
of the iron fence five red fingers
flashing like a cardinal in the snow.

Ohio

I could spend my time driving
from motel to motel, sleeping always
in the stale chambers of the disappeared.

The second book

Every object in creation is you, every
tree, flower, bud, child, every bright window,
every creature slaloming around the night trees.

Why we are sometimes silent

> The solitude of your fall is terrible
> in the weak sun of a winter afternoon—
> far away a friend turned back, saw.

Lear howls

Never, never, never, never, never—
five perfect trochees of helpless defiance.
Always is no opposite of this never.

Still winter

No booms of cracking ice,
no rush of torrent sweeping away bridges.
I knew spring would bring more quiet.

Graveyard in winter

I cannot think of your cold body.
I cannot in the snow not think
of you there in the cold forever.

Prayer

Let the ice melt apace without irony
Let lilacs bloom in the dead earth
Let sweet showers outrun my grief

No more seasons

March will come as it always does
and spring and summer behind like dolls
within dolls opening the shrinking future.

April snow

So what if it's spring? Let it snow,
let it snow till June. My daughter
is dead and no good lies ahead.

Et in arcadia ego

Why carry on because spring has come?
Is my flesh grass? Although yours is,
I continue in this illusion of life.

Weeding

It's filthy digging down in the dirt,
tugging on roots too deep to unearth,
crushing the crumblings of last year.

Four elements

In the pouring down of fiery spring
you were covered in white pear blossoms
blowing like snow, smelling like wet.

Would you mind

I am writing the world without you,
trying to relearn leaves, verbs,
my own hands, our future?

Visitors

Your friends saw us through this year.
They came to say goodbye with food,
their black hair shining in the night.

Library solstice

The last time books shone in June,
the evening light striking their dark spines,
you were coming home to us soon.

A shaft from possibility

In the slant of evening sun,
down a narrow shady sidewalk,
my daughter chases dust motes.

Afterword

When I was a student, English teachers always made us memorize lines of poetry, lines from Shakespeare, Donne, Dickinson, Frost. They said there would be a time when we would need these lines. They did not dream of Google or Smart Phones making every line ever written available immediately. They lived in a world of typewriters; poetry was meant for moments of crisis, public and private, when the oral tradition might become necessary.

When my daughter died, I joined the company of every parent who has outlived her child. I wished never to have learned how welcoming fellow mourners could be, but I joined them willingly, met them in coffee shops and sought them out in anthologies and on websites. I knew that others in my and my husband's family had lost children. They were silent; there was a mostly repressed oral tradition, an undercover history of trauma— one was hit by a car at three; another backed out of a tailor's window at twenty—but no written messages from the mothers and fathers.

I found some poems written by parents—Ben Jonson, William Wordsworth, Victor Hugo, Jan Kochanowski, Robert Frost— grandparents—Anne Bradstreet—even by siblings—Catullus, Seamus Heaney and Anne Carson—but most of the poems of mourning I read were by spouses or children, lovers or friends. In the death of a child there is something unspeakable, something that reduces us all to the silence of Lear's "Never, never, never, never, never." King Lear dies, but most of us live on having to speak and look and smell and touch as well as to howl and weep.

These poems contain many allusions to other poets. Remembered lines attached themselves to images and new meanings flew out. Frost's "Home Burial" or Poe's "Annabel Lee," a fragment of Sappho or a phrase from Shakespeare made a different kind of sense to me now. Auden's "Funeral Blues," which somehow I had never read before that summer, let me know it was okay to feel what I was feeling.

I started writing brief three-line poems about a month after Rachel died. I first put them together into a sequence around the anniversary of her accident, death and burial. I wrote them because I somehow had to understand the world anew.

A native New Yorker, **Katherine Barrett Swett** has a PhD in American Literature from Columbia University and heads the English Department at an independent school. She lives with her husband and two sons in New York. Her poems have appeared recently in *The Lyric* and *Rattle*.

CPSIA information can be obtained
at www.ICGtesting.com
Printed in the USA
LVOW07s0053040117
519651LV00004B/112/P